Do It Write Math

by Toni Jones

World Teachers Press

Published with the permission of R.I.C. Publications Pty. Ltd.

Copyright © 1997 by Didax, Inc., Rowley, MA 01969. All rights reserved.

First published by R.I.C. Publications Pty. Ltd., Perth, Western Australia.

Limited reproduction permission: The publisher grants permission to individual teachers who have purchased this book to reproduce the blackline masters as needed for use with their own students. Reproduction for an entire school or school district or for commercial use is prohibited.

Printed in the United States of America.

Order Number 2-5032
ISBN 1-885111-45-2

A B C D E F 97 98 99 00

395 Main Street
Rowley, MA 01969

Foreword

This book contains a variety of hands-on mathematical activities. These activities cover the number, space and measurement strands of the mathematics syllabus. An icon at the top of each page denotes which strand the activity applies to:

N = Number   **S** = Space   **M** = Measurement

Materials needed for each activity are clearly listed at the top of each worksheet, making organization easy.

A question has been provided at the bottom of most pages to allow students to communicate or report their conclusions and consolidate the focus of the lesson. This also allows students to develop the mathematical ideas further and the teacher to assess each student's progress.

These activities have been designed to use with small groups, large groups, or as individual lessons taught at the point of need.

Table of Contents

Worksheet	Kind	Page
Foreword and Table of Contents		3
Teacher Information		4-5
Start to Finish	Measurement	6
Making Triangles	Space	7
Geoboard Touch	Space	8
Rubber Band Geo	Space	9
Pattern Blocks	Space	10
Fill the Pattern	Space	11
Most and Least	Space	12
Cover with Five	Space	13
Cover with Six	Space	14
Patterns with Shapes	Space	15
Creature Creation	Number	16
Space Creature	Space	17
Pattern Shapes	Number	18
Three Bears	Number	19
Number Puzzle	Number	20
Addition Magician	Number	21

Worksheet	Kind	Page
Towers	Number	22
Stringy String	Measurement	23
Perimeter Pal	Space/Measurement	24
Surface Blobs	Space/Measurement	25
Ordinal Positions	Number	26
Treasure Hunt	Number	27
Monster Chase	Number	28
Where's the Bear?	Number	29
Centi-spider	Measurement	30
What Shape am I?	Space	31
Ticktock	Measurement	32
Egg Cartons	Number	33
Symmetrical Shapes	Space	34
Problem Solving	Number	35
Caterpillar Math	Number	36
Color the Flowers	Number	37
Smallest to Biggest	Measurement	38
Class Graphing	Measurement	39

Teacher Information

Introduction

It is recognized that the linking of curriculum areas is beneficial to the development of young children. 'Do it Write Math' provides the opportunity for teachers to link two important areas of the curriculum into one activity. These two areas are activity-based math and language.

The thirty-four activities in this book follow a similar format, while developing a wide range of mathematical concepts from the areas of number, space and measurement. Each activity includes the following components.

Materials

Materials to be used are presented in pictorial and written form. This allows for opportunity to discuss the materials, their construction and application and then to introduce the words into the vocabulary of the students. This way, the language being used becomes an integral part of the lesson.

Instruction

Instructions for the activity are simple, easy to follow and generally require the student to provide a response based on their findings. This provides further opportunity to discuss and introduce new language to the student's vocabulary.

Conclusion

This is a vital part of the lesson from both a mathematical and language perspective.

Mathematically, this part of the lesson provides an opportunity for the teacher and students to focus on the main concept of the lesson (what did we learn today), and also to discuss developments that occurred outside the specific objective.

In terms of language, this part of the lesson provides opportunity for students to verbally and in written form provide feedback and a review of the lesson. Often from this teachers can identify the development of misconceptions as well as the successful development of a concept.

The focus of all the activities in this book is to investigate mathematics in a practical manner and to develop language skills through the introduction of new vocabulary and written and verbal communication skills.

Example Lesson Development

Activity Start to Finish - Page 6

Introductory Work Each activity develops a basic mathematical concept. When introducing the activity, discussion should relate to real life examples and comparisons so students can relate to what is being taught. Focus should also be placed on how language, both written and verbal, will play an important part in the lesson.

Development The following are features of the activity that can assist in getting the most from the worksheet.

1. **Materials**
   Discuss the materials shown and what their uses are. Also include the words as part of the students word bank if applicable.

2. **Instructions**
   Have students read instructions out loud and then discuss what is being requested. Focus on students who are unclear on what is required.

3. **Answers**
   Encourage students to be clear with their answers and not to write until they are sure.

4. **Conclusion**
   This is very important for students to reflect on the problems and success of the activity and to communicate in written form.

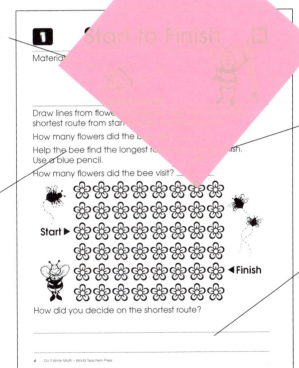

Extension Extension of the concept is possible through further measurement and number activities. The remaining activities in the book will further develop the language/math link that is the focus of the lessons.

Start to Finish

Materials:

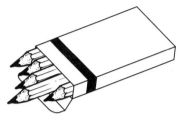

colored pencils

Draw lines from flower to flower to help the bee find the shortest route from start to finish. Use a red pencil.

How many flowers did the bee visit? _____

Help the bee find the longest route from start to finish. Use a blue pencil.

How many flowers did the bee visit? _____

How did you decide on the shortest route?

_____

_____

2 Making Triangles S

Materials:

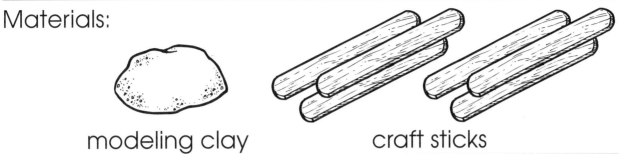

modeling clay   craft sticks

Use six sticks to make a triangle.
Draw a picture of your triangle.

Use five sticks to make a triangle.
Draw a picture of your triangle.

What did you find out?

_____

_____

3 Geoboard Touch

Materials:

geoboard   rubber bands

Use two rubber bands to make this shape on the geoboard.

How many nails do the rubber bands touch?

_____

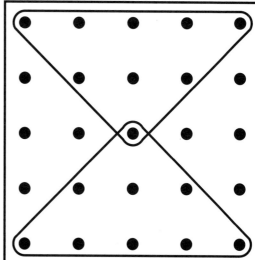

Make your own shape using two rubber bands. Draw your shape on the geoboard.

How many nails do the rubber bands touch?

_____

What did you find out?

_____

8 Do It Write Math – World Teachers Press

4 Rubber Band Geo S

Materials:

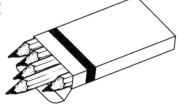
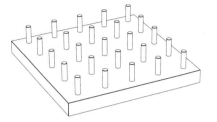
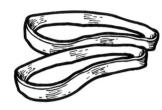

colored pencils   geoboard   rubber bands

1. Use two rubber bands to make three squares on the board. Draw the squares on the geoboard in green pencil.

2. Use two rubber bands to make three rectangles on the board. Draw the figures on the geoboard in red pencil.

3. Use two rubber bands to make two squares and a rectangle. Draw the figures on the geoboard in blue pencil.

4. Use two rubber bands to make three triangles on the board. Draw the figures on the geoboard in yellow pencil.

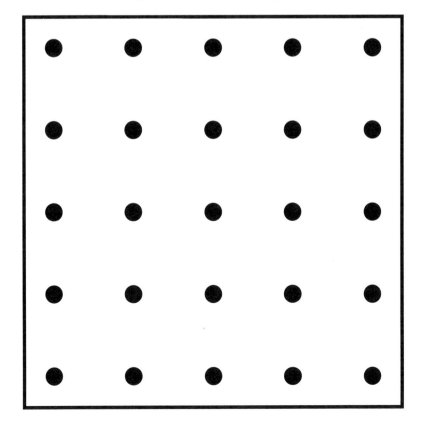

Do It Write Math – World Teachers Press

Pattern Blocks

Materials: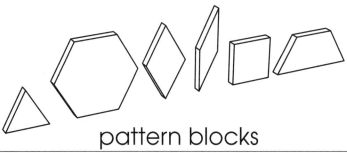
pattern blocks

1. Make an animal using pattern blocks.
   Draw a picture of your animal.

2. Make a flower using pattern blocks.
   Draw a picture of the flower.

Write about your animal.

_____

_____

_____

Fill the Pattern

Materials: pattern blocks

Cover these shapes using the pattern blocks.

How many pattern blocks did you use? ☐

How many different shapes did you use? ☐

How many pattern blocks did you use? ☐

How many different shapes did you use? ☐

Is there more than one way to do this? _____

Explain. _____

7 Most and Least

Materials: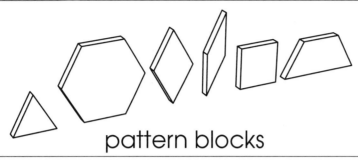
pattern blocks

Fill these shapes using as many blocks as you can.

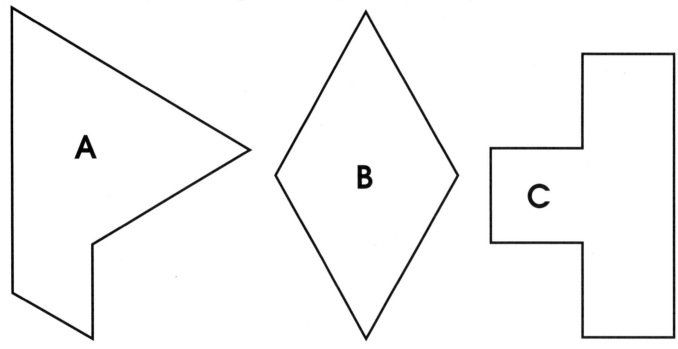

I used _____ _____ _____

Now fill the shapes using as few blocks as you can.

I used _____ _____ _____

What did you find out?

_____

_____

Cover with Five

Materials: pattern blocks

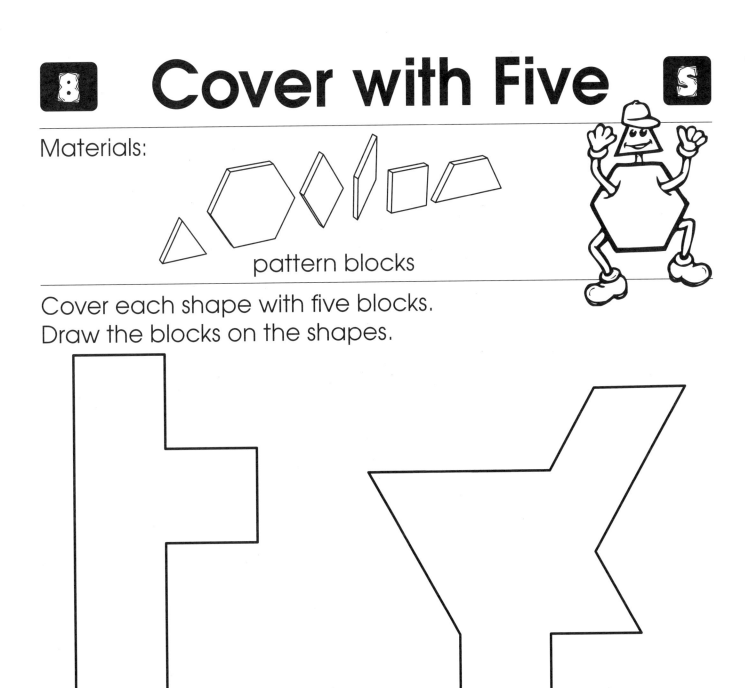

Cover each shape with five blocks.
Draw the blocks on the shapes.

What did you find out?

_____

_____

Do It Write Math – World Teachers Press

Cover with Six

Materials:

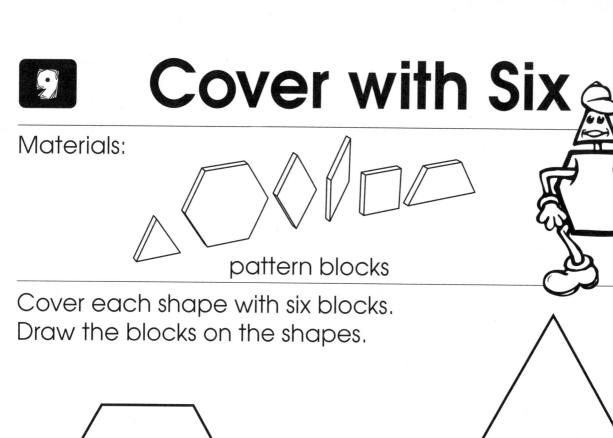

pattern blocks

Cover each shape with six blocks.
Draw the blocks on the shapes.

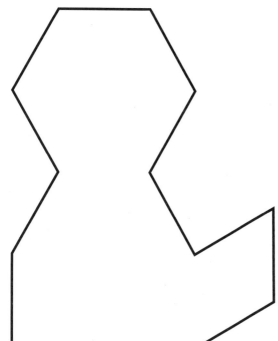

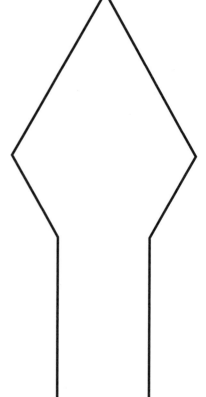

What did you find out?

10 Patterns with Shapes

Materials:

pattern blocks

Finish the patterns. Draw the missing shapes.

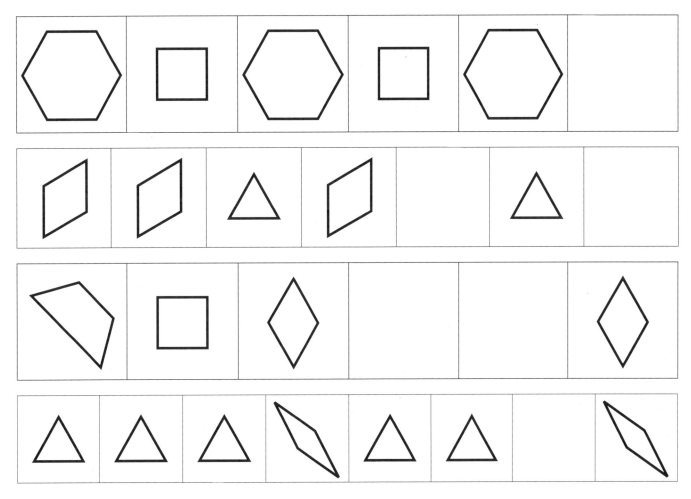

How did you decide on the missing pieces?

_____

_____

11 Creature Creation

Materials:

colored pencils

Using the shape below create a deci-beast!
Give your beast ten eyes and ten legs.
When you have finished color your creature.

Describe your deci-beast.

_____

_____

_____

Space Creature

Materials:

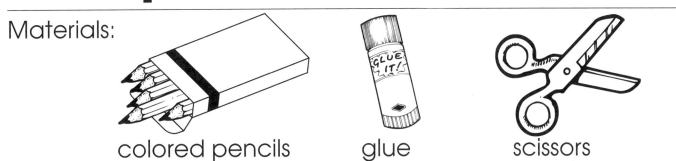

colored pencils · glue · scissors

Cut out the shapes below and create an animal or space creature. Add eyes, a nose and a mouth.

13 Pattern Shapes

Materials:

colored pencils   scissors

Cut out and color these shapes to make a pattern. Describe your pattern.

_____

_____

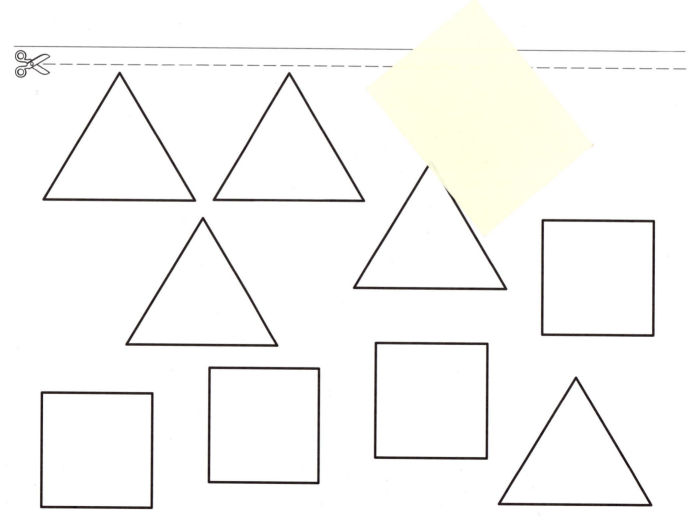

Three Bears

Materials:

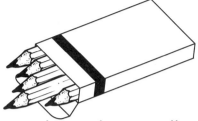
colored pencils

Use three different colored pencils to color the bears below. Give each bear a different colored head, shirt and pants.

How did you do it?

___

___

___

Do It Write Math – World Teachers Press

Number Puzzle

Materials:
scissors

1. Cut out the four pieces below.
2. Fit the pieces together to make a square which adds up to eight on each side.

How did you solve the number puzzle?

___

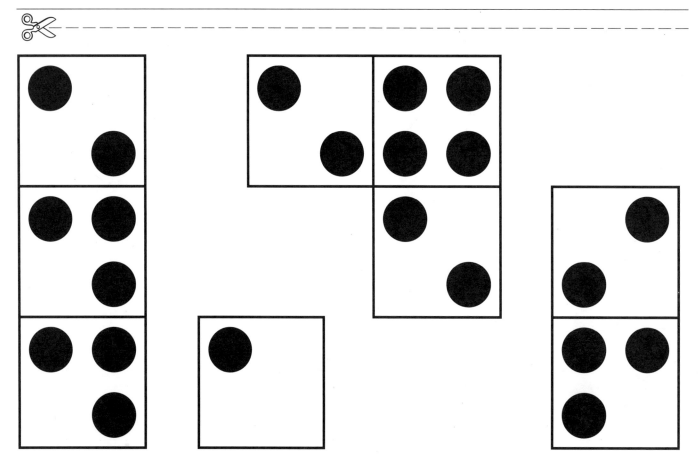

Addition Magician

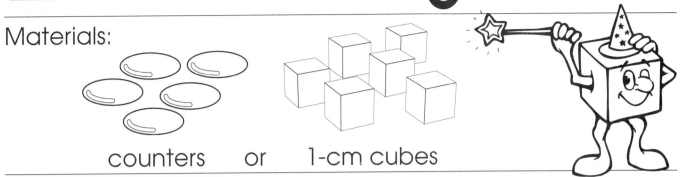

Materials: counters or 1-cm cubes

Use the numbers below to find as many pairs as you can that add up to 18.

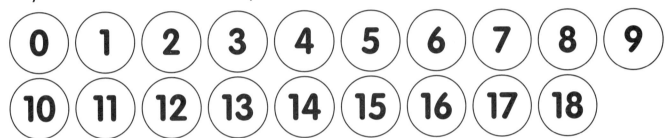

Write the numbers in the circles.

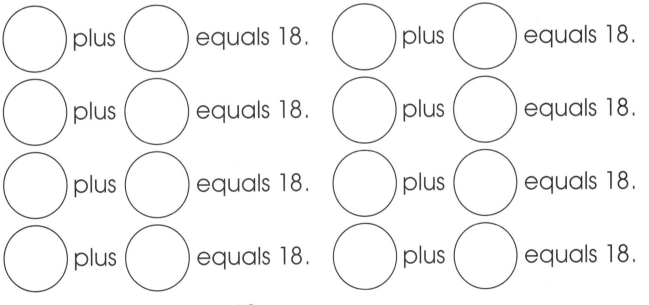

◯ plus ◯ equals 18.   ◯ plus ◯ equals 18.

◯ plus ◯ equals 18.   ◯ plus ◯ equals 18.

◯ plus ◯ equals 18.   ◯ plus ◯ equals 18.

◯ plus ◯ equals 18.   ◯ plus ◯ equals 18.

What did you find out?

Towers

Materials: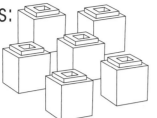
interlocking cubes   colored pencils

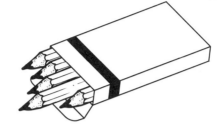

Using only 2 different colors of interlocking cubes, build a tower 10 cubes high.

Example: 2 red + 5 blue + 3 red = 10 cubes

Show your tower below by coloring the squares. Make up some other combinations and show them too.

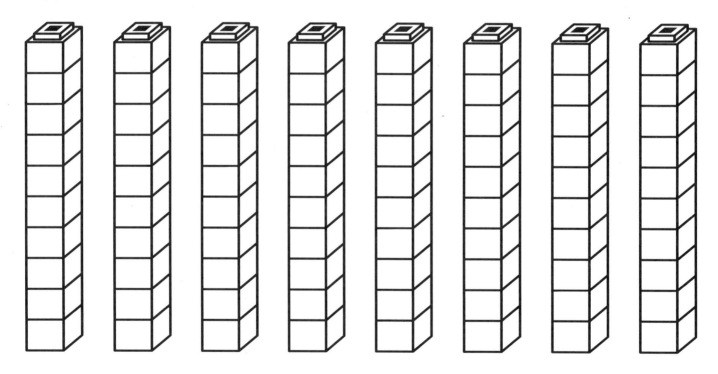

What did you find out?

_____

_____

Stringy String

Materials:

string   glue   scissors

Measure the following things and cut a piece of string the same size.

  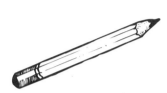 

a crayon   a pencil   a finger

Glue the strings from shortest to longest below:

Shortest
Longest

What did you find out?

Do It Write Math – World Teachers Press

19 Perimeter Pal

Materials:

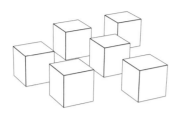
1-cm cubes

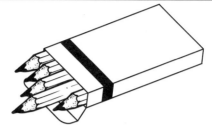
colored pencils

Use 1-cm cubes to measure the perimeter of this shape.

Write your answer below.

The perimeter of the rectangle is

_____ cubes.

Use a colored pencil to show the perimeter of the shape.
What does perimeter mean?

_____

_____

_____

20 Surface Blobs

Materials:

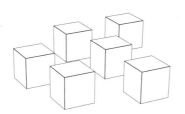
1-cm cubes

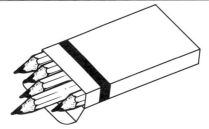
colored pencils

Cover the blobs below with 1-cm cubes to see how many cubes it takes to fill the whole surface area.

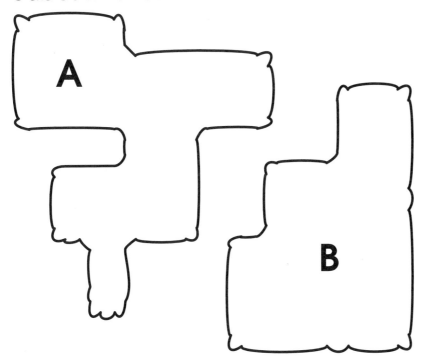

Write your answer below.
The surface area of blob A is

_____ cubes.

The surface area of the blob B is

_____ cubes.

Use a colored pencil to show the surface area of the shapes.

What does surface area mean?

_____

_____

Do It Write Math – World Teachers Press 25

21 Ordinal Positions

1. Color the first star.

2. Color the fifth square.

3. Color the fourth cat.

4. Color the second triangle.

5. Color the first and fifth cars.

6. Color the ninth and tenth apples.

7. I have ☐ brothers and sisters. I am the ☐ child in my family.

When do we use ordinal numbers? _____

Treasure Hunt

Count by twos to find the treasure.
Color the path as you go.

2	4	5
1	6	7

10	13	12	10	8	9
15	16	14	20	13	11
19	18	20
17	16	19

Can you find a pattern in the numbers counting by twos?

Monster Chase

Count by fives to catch the monster. Color the path as you go.

When would you need to count by fives?

_____

_____

24 Where's the Bear?

Count by tens to find the bear.
Color the path as you go.

When would you need to count by tens?

___

Centi-spider

Materials:

scissors

things to measure

Cut out the spider ruler at the bottom of the page and use it to measure the items listed below.

How many centi-spiders long is…

1. your book? _____ centi-spiders.

2. your desk? _____ centi-spiders.

3. the back of your chair? _____ centi-spiders.

4. your pencil? _____ centi-spiders.

5. your hand? _____ centi-spiders.

6. your scissors? _____ centi-spiders.

7. one math cube? _____ centi-spiders.

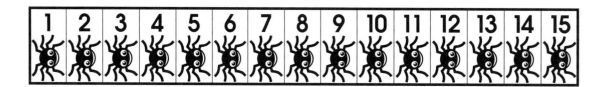

26 What Shape am I?

Read the clues below. Name and draw the shapes.

1. I have three sides and no curves.
   I also have three angles.

   What shape am I?

2. I have two long equal sides and two short equal sides. All my sides are straight and all of my angles are the same.

   What shape am I?

3. I have six equal sides and six corners. All of my sides are straight and all of my angles are the same.

   What shape am I?

4. I have no straight sides. I measure the same from my middle to my outside all the way round.

   What shape am I?

Ticktock

27 M

What time is on the clocks?
Write down what you do at these times.

Time ____ : ____

What I do: _____
_____
_____
_____
_____

Time ____ : ____

What I do: _____
_____
_____
_____
_____

Time ____ : ____

What I do: _____
_____
_____
_____
_____

Time ____ : ____

What I do: _____
_____
_____
_____
_____

How does telling the time help us?

_____

28 Egg Cartons

Materials:

half egg carton

3 red cubes

3 blue cubes

Arrange the colored cubes in half an egg carton, by placing one cube in each space. There are many different combinations.

Find 6 different combinations.
Draw and color them in the cartons below.

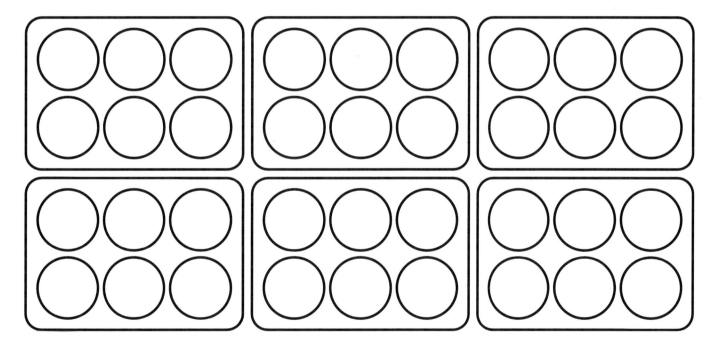

What did you find out?

29 Symmetrical Shapes

Draw a line down the middle of these shapes to show that they are symmetrical.

What does symmetrical mean?

___

___

___

Now draw some of your own symmetrical shapes.

30 Problem Solving

Solve these problems. Draw a picture and write a number sentence for each problem.

1. Jane has 14 pencils. She gave four away. How many does she have now?

   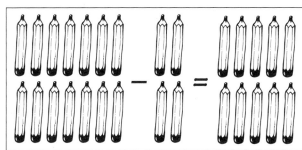

   _____

2. Martin had 12 pencils. He wanted to give them all to four of his friends. How many would each get?

   _____

3. There are three girls with two bows each in their hair. How many bows are there in all?

   _____

4. Write your own problem to go with this number sentence:

   4 x 2 =

   _____

   _____

31 Caterpillar Math

Add up the numbers in each segment of the caterpillar. Write the total inside the small circle without using your calculator.

Then use your calculator to add up the entire caterpillar.

Did you find any short-cuts?

32 Color the Flowers

Materials:

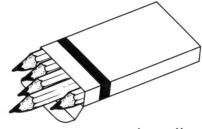

red, blue, green and yellow pencils

Use these clues to help you decide what colors the flowers should be.

1. The first flower is not red and is not next to the red flower.
2. The third flower is not next to the yellow flower.
3. The fourth flower is not red.
4. The second flower is not blue.

Which flower did you color first? _____

Why? _____

Smallest to Biggest

Materials:

scissors   glue

Cut out the footprints below and glue them from smallest to biggest.

How did you find out which footprint was the smallest?

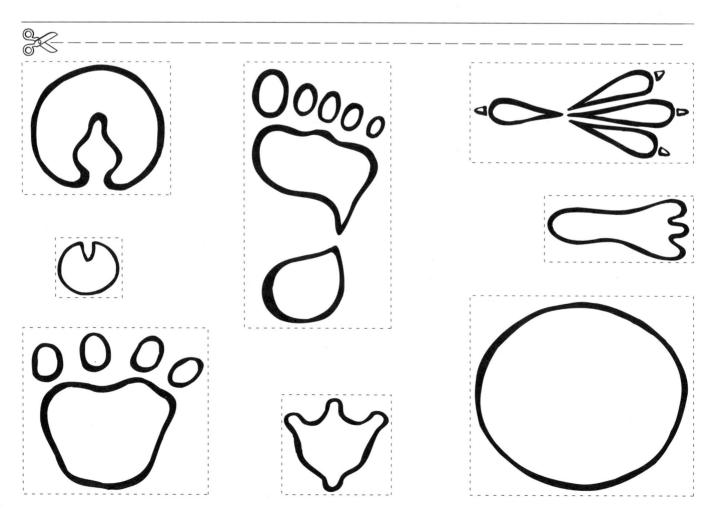

34 Class Graphing

Use the graph below to record how many people in your class have blond hair, brown hair, black hair or red hair. If someone in your class doesn't have any of these colors then record their hair color in the 'other' boxes.

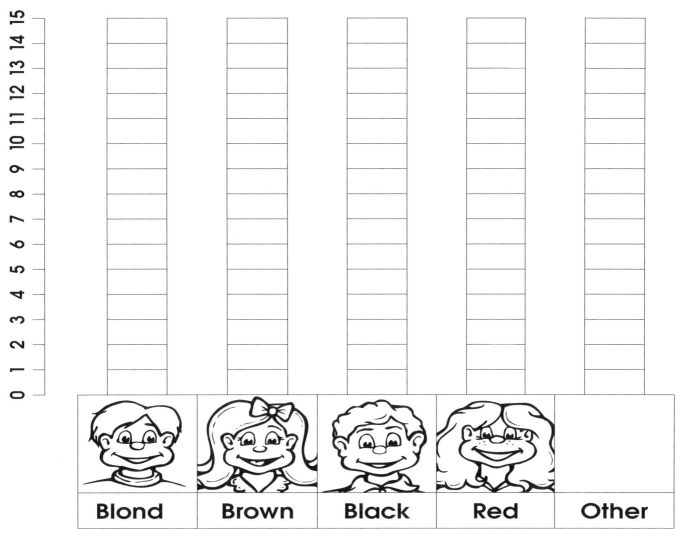

What did you find out?

_____

_____

_____

About the Author

UNITED STATES OF AMERICA

Toni Jones, Oklahoma, USA.
Toni is originally from the United States and has taught in primary schools in both Australia and the U.S. She specializes in teaching lower elementary grades and her books present practical, easy-to-use activities that link major subject areas with a special focus on integrating language into all curriculum areas. Her wide range of teaching experience is reflected in the universal appeal of her work.